Fire on Water

Also by Colleen Keating and published by Ginninderra Press
A Call To Listen
(Shortlisted, Society of Women Writers NSW Book Awards 2016)

Colleen Keating

Fire on Water

Acknowledgements

Some of the poems in this book have won awards:
'In Search of Hildegard of Bingen' was a finalist in the Dame Mary Gilmore Poetry Award for the 90th anniversary of the Society of Women Writers NSW 2016, inspired by the theme Giving Women a Voice.
'Wood pigeon (for yana)' was First in the *Positive Words* Annual Poetry Competition 2015.
'Hydra' was Second in the FreeXpresSion Poetry Competition 2015.

Many of the poems have appeared in publications, including *Eureka Street, The Mozzie, Poetry Matters, The Good Oil* (SGS), *FreeXpresSion, Winning Ways* and *Womens Ink*.
I am grateful to the editors for their encouragement and dedication to poetry.

Some poems have also appeared in the following anthologies:
Bare: An anthology of poetry and prose (Women Writers Network, 2015)
Inner Child (Poetica Christi Press, 2015)
'This poem is about silence', from my first collection *A Call to Listen*, appeared in *First Refuge* (edited by Ann Nadge, Ginninderra Press, 2016)

I would like to thank the co-convenors Sue Good and Annie Ayers and the members of the Women Writers Network, and Norm Neill and fellow poets of the Wednesday Evening Poetry group at NSW Writers Centre, Rozelle, for their positive critique, affirmation and keeping me on task.
Appreciation to Decima Wraxall for her friendship and support.

Thank you to Margaret Hede and Michael Keating
for the final edit of my work.

My loving appreciation to Michael
for his constant presence and inspiration

Fire on Water
ISBN 978 1 76041 351 4
Copyright © text Colleen Keating 2017
Cover image: Elizabeth Keating-Jones

First published 2017 by
GINNINDERRA PRESS
PO Box 3461 Port Adelaide 5015 Australia
www.ginninderrapress.com.au

Contents

Fire on Water	9
forever	11
darginyung	12
awakening	13
out of a black sea	14
lesson learnt	15
after the storm	16
reflection	17
waiting	18
phantoms	19
fire on water	20
at The Entrance	21
dervish dancer	24
a love letter	25
the dream	26
surfboard rider	27
seeing eyes	28
shadows ripples whispers	29
galloping sea	30
lake poem	32
Where's Home, Ulysses?	33
where's home ulysses?	35
farewell beautiful home	36
downsizing	38
banana boxes	40
belongings	41
new bush track	42
traces of you	44
first morning in our new home	45

Lie of the Land — 47

- lie of the land — 49
- forgotten warriors — 50
- Multuggerah — 52
- battle of Richmond Hill — 53
- first executions in Melbourne — 54
- Jandamarra — 56

Requiem for Bees — 57

- where have the tiny birds gone — 59
- lamentation — 60
- remembering — 61
- heart song — 62
- in search of Hildegard of Bingen — 63
- requiem for bees — 66
- a flight of fancy — 67

Counting Dead Women — 69

- forgotten children — 71
- counting dead women — 72
- common denominator — 73
- secret history — 74
- stillborn — 75
- fear of lack — 76
- empathy — 77
- so what! — 78
- out of sight out of mind — 80
- please call me by my name — 81
- we are sorry — 82
- the wrong side of the track — 83
- hydra — 84
- christmas is over — 86

Eagle Wings — 87

- on becoming a grandparent — 89
- distant grandparenting — 90
- 3 moments at Heathrow — 91
- spirit guide — 92
- witness — 94
- refuge — 95
- weeping day — 96
- eagle wings — 97
- claustrophobic — 98
- waking to day — 99
- bucket list — 100
- funeral for a lover of Italian travel — 101

Exultation — 103

- parallel realms — 105
- not narcissus — 106
- taking wings — 107
- choice — 108
- sunflowers — 109
- the vicissitude of a blue butterfly — 110
- exultation — 111
- autumnal music — 112
- red sirens — 113
- for a moment — 114
- wood pigeon — 115
- in our garden — 116
- old violin — 117
- visitor — 118
- Rostropovich — 119
- unexpected visitor — 120
- a poem of instruction — 121

Fire on Water

forever

for Michael

caught in the gossamer of the moment
wrapped in seductive arms
we yarned and sang   ate marshmallows
danced   soaked in laughing rains and played
with rainbows   frolicked naked in the sea
loved setting suns   drank wine to the moon
thought   this is forever

and dared a skerrick of doubt to creep in

darginyung

welcome to country   drones
        the didgeridoo   its spirit
                circles the hollowed wood

sings the darkness into dawn
        and in its dancing rhythm
                the dreaming drifts in

awakening

when i hear words like this
there appears to be new texture
even birdsong seems elevated

when i hear words like this
it occurs to me the dawn has an aureate glow
that the ocean sings in celebration

a heart on mute   beats again
on pause   wings again

from heart to heart like music in a round
into every dark corner like sparrows in a thorn bush
people will feel the chalice of humanity again
that is their gift to the world

out of a black sea

i face the dark
question the point of writing any more

the horizon stirs
out of a black sea

a hula-hoop dancer
spins out
circles a muted sky

spangles a corrugated-silver sea
sends out ripples of laughter
tickles sombre clouds
silhouettes
the quiet breathing palms

an aspirant to great heights
she climbs
dizzily intoxicated

and reaches out to me
still at the window
with tiny blissful pieces of inspiration

lesson learnt

first rule   when questing for the poetic
on a tidal line of an ocean rock ledge
watch for the rogue wave

it is not recommended to lie on the barnacled edge
of a scalloped moon-shaped rock pool
as you wait on its mystery   and watch
your reflection in azure sky
with clustered clouds
like empty thought bubbles
around you   fill with deep secrets

the second rule is to keep your wits
do not get lost in an inner realm
as you can in a Beethoven symphony

it is not recommended to become immersed
in tapestry of colours shimmered by the sea

in the light among the stones   drum-shaped chitons
clustered iridescent stars and speckled shells
a venetian-red anemone flirting like a solitary flute
black spiky urchins and the wait for the shy crab
to scuttle out from the king neptune necklace

it is all too hypnotic

the lesson learnt
expect the unexpected

after the storm

on the rocky ledge she stands
confronts the crashing waves
that roar in like tigers
to devour her

she reads the weather like one reads maps
whip of wind wildly plays in her hair
sting of salt on her fresh red cheeks
a smile on her face

reflection

remote pond –
her worries sink from her mind
into sediment

waiting

tripod planted firmly in the sand
lens uncapped

i glance around to see her focus

could it be dawn colours
that still linger

the ocean's unruly tangle
or rainbow mist that wings its way
where ocean and rocks surge

i catch pelicans skating in
to wait near a fisherman

watch the light dance
along spindrift of waves

see a hawk hover on the wind
a patient wait for prey

there is an extravagance
about this morning to be savoured

then i see a surfer on her board
facing the curl of the sea
running its curve
as the photographer
catches her
catching the wave

phantoms

look out towards the ocean
see the morning fog tease the horizon
see it stretch

waft   stealthily
drift into the day
devour the sea   sky   lake   sand

a pelican flying by
comes out like a phantom
and disappears as if it never was

a drizzly ball of sun eight a.m. high
smiles in battle
knowing its heat will be the victor

this is not the misty edge of avalon
'tis a mystical beach on the central coast
on a foggy summer morning

come   walk along the beach
as each damp white-hemmed wave
ripples around our bare feet

in this moist briny air
you and i are also phantoms
we need to touch to know we are here

fire on water

from a lilac sky   clouds
full with the sheen of red taffeta
like flaming bubbles of thought

become balls of fire
on water

some might declare this a miracle
enough for me
to be alive in this moment

at The Entrance

dawn stirs the big space of sea
sky drizzles a coloured potion
over the navy night

along the winter beach
the constant ebb and flow of waves splurge

a solitary fishermen   on the rocky outcrop at Karangi Point
stands above the shoaling waves of the channel
as it races out to sea

back on the sand
a photographer catches the moment

walkers   along the boardwalk
take in the sun as it skims across the ocean
and accompanies them on their way
some stride out   joggers surge past

two in wetsuits with surfboards
sprint down to the fiery sea

the winking Norah Head lighthouse
like a shift worker goes to sleep

sphinx-like on the headland
the old lifesaving clubhouse
has a whitewash dulux glow

blocks of units   most with blinds still closed
against early glare   wait
with empty balconies and promise of blue views

along the esplanade   over Fishermen's Wharf
under the bridge   past the boat shed
with its boats for hire and always fishy smell
the pelican-sprawled lake
now fierce-punctured with sun shards
has a hectic restless veneer

its surface tussles with itself
each lap   greedy
as the first motorboats set out
to their bombora fishing grounds

further out on the lake   paradox of black swans
with their necks curled away
move as lullaby music

beyond them   the Wattigan Mountains
stand as blue denim sentinels

above on the phosphate-denuded branches of Norfolk Pines
some cormorants still hang out
others already diving for breakfast below

flocks of oystercatchers go south for the day
sea gulls squabble
pelicans wait patiently by the boat ramp
for fishermen to return

near the waterline   unblemished sand
waits for the first footprints of the day

back a little   on the dry sand
camouflaged sand crabs   dart
as if playing games with my shadow

in a sand buggy   the lifesavers
ride down to the beach   check the surf
place the distinctive red and yellow flags

and the day has began

dervish dancer

the sea today fills me with its flounce
it shimmers   a flamboyant crowd of bling

like an eccentric retiree with nothing to lose
and yet caught   losing everything

the horizon comes up closer
stares me in the face

there is no stopping it coming closer

the sea in her divinity
washes the feet of every shore

swirling her skirts like a dervish dancer
her service is evocative

she lulls and sings and serves
sometimes with laughter and joy

sometimes with deep wails and sobs

a love letter

lines in the sand
curl with each wave

like ocean thoughts
their swash is punctuated

with grit and shell and weed
sometimes an odd treasure
words i cannot read
interpreting them only from sound

i hear sorrow and triumph
serenading me to love

and seduced   my bare toes
scribble a love letter in reply

the dream

cool salty water
washing around my body
to refresh   renew
washing through every cell
to energise   vitalise

putting on my swimmers
gathering my cap and goggles
i gaze out
the ocean rolling in
never ceases to amaze

this is the dream
that got me up today

surfboard rider

hazy with distance
speck of a human being

in an untamed wilderness
the sheer beauty
of this endeavour
refracted in millions of silver shards

seeing eyes

sitting on his balcony
with a bird's-eye view
full of ocean and sky
he was master
synchronising the tides with his routine
keeping check on pelican politics
the lowdown on seagull squabbles
he could give the lakeside fishermen
a valued word or two

i learnt from shared observations
how many whales have gone north
how many return
where the rips are
where the surfboard riders should be
to catch the best

as he watched the horizon
did he notice it closing in
tiptoeing like an evening tide

now   down an institutional corridor
four walls hold him
white gowns rush about
with not even the sound of a crying gull

don't worry   he says
i have seeing eyes
and my mind has wings
i'll always be there

shadows ripples whispers

beach walking
not alone
loyal shadow

tiny fish
ripple the surface
water's thoughts

inner child
whispers from dimness of time
play play play

galloping sea

all day the ocean gallops
in pursuit of the super moon
even at its ebb it has an untamed canter
it bolts over the rocky bombora
spindrift like a wild tail flares
golden   as it catches the evening light

at night   here we are   what a combination
a frisky sea and a frisky moon
greedily taking colour from all around
no room to fray at the edges here

such enchantment
the world that lays itself out for pleasure
seduces   delights

there is something bigger at play
do you hear it calling
will you arise
brave the wind
cover up from the chill
walk with me

the news gives me a sense of free fall
it bombards our airwaves
with wars ramped up
pockmarking our small blue planet

yet the ocean calls
its waves lift and curl
as if to enfold us
the sand bears its soul

this super moon
gives its light generously
its beauty unsurpassed

lake poem

dawn catches little terns across a playground
of sandy islands   the lake

changes its face with the vacillating light
a thousand water stars twinkle

the little terns have arrived for the summer
vibrant visitors from the north   they will nest

on the shores   and swoop and soar for hours
energetic displays to ward off aggressors

at high tide   the islands
lift off   a cacophony of wings

in a fluster to the beach sand
a pelican cruises perusing crowded footholds

in the Norfolk Pines the cormorants hang out
the seagulls squabble for every space

a breeze zigzags the afternoon lake
reeds sway around the new signs to *keep dogs*

at all times on a leash   with the late afternoon light
a willow-blue sky blushes   sun slips past the hills

the lake like porcelain   mirrors the sky
ready for its jewelled decoration of night stars

Where's Home, Ulysses?

where's home ulysses?*

my mind shuffles like an untidy bookcase
my hands hold an inventory of my life
over boxes labelled   in   out

it is called downsizing   decluttering
some call it simplifying   culling

where there is a home
make a house   depersonalise
the real estate agent says

ebay   vinnies   salvos
devour my story
on the footpath   garbage pick-up
my life exposed

there is an ithaca touch of lostness
in this adventure
except I hope the road is short

where's home ulysses?

* Judith Wright

farewell beautiful home

a white house high on the rise
at its front door
an irish welcome waits
and an assuring worn sign
angels guard this house

in a quiet cul-de-sac
set amongst five rare Sydney blue gums
that nest rainbow lorikeets
rest sulphur-crested cockatoos   galahs   crows
with night tracks for possums and brush turkey
branches for discerning kookaburras
that laugh and laugh
often when we are
full of self-importance
and chortling magpies
with a song as steeped in our psyche
as a well brewed pot of tea

this home   reared six children
and for the past fourteen years
millie   the superior labrador
always on guard   and chair
of the welcoming committee
for friends to arrive and family to return

we are saying farewell beautiful home
we have shared a rich story
like a good chat that you don't want to end
every room has its own conversation

our stewardship is over
gardens   gutters   fences   plumbing and cleaning
for over forty years
children have their own homes
millie her job complete has passed gracefully

now space for a new story

downsizing

how agreeable it is   not to be staying forever in the family home
guarding her memories and being the tender keeper of her story
how much better   to strike out into unfamiliar territory
letting go of what still claims part of you   sacred   precious
feeling uncertainty tug

walls of family photos tell of celebrations and milestones
forty years to create   only an hour to take down
and now a blank wall negates the history
books are unnecessary with Google and Kindle and iPad even though
books are your life and they give wings to your heart

instead of soil behind fingernails and down on stiff knees
smelling compost and moist earth and though the vegie and herb patch
garden of blue gums and birds nurtures your soul
who wants all that constant work of falling twigs   leaves and seed pods
in a diminished world you can sip coffee and just watch

your crazy social justice wall erased by the window cleaner
doesn't erase passion
and why are there shelves of videos pre-loved   and unplayable

decluttering hurts like little deaths and fondling treasures in one's hand
for the last time and choosing salvos or out bin

is like losing a little of oneself
it shocks mortality out of its pigeonhole where it was kept buried

the conveyor belt of change builds to a loud rumbling sound
choices narrow like a funnel's choking neck but

the vinyls are staying   i mightn't be able to play them
but i choose to keep sleeves with young faces of leonard cohen
joni mitchell   bob dylan and the seekers smiling out at me

i might even update the record player
and on my new terrace   take time to relax and listen

banana boxes

all the boxes have been used
and the last books need to be packed

free from Coles
given with a smile by a young man

four banana boxes
sturdy   slip over lids

slight smell of banana
a few remnants of dry black skin

bananas to books

as i pack i ponder change

let it be for me   renaissance
may i be as accepting
as these boxes

belongings

*angels can fly because they take themselves lightly**

my arms and heart   were full
with belongings
when we downsized from the family home

we rented a garage   and filled it
letting go was not an option
so I locked them away

sometimes when I visited
it began to look unneeded
nothing called at me

one day   my heart unlocked
i donated some and ordered a skip
emptied the garage   returned the key

it felt like a heavy pack moved
off my back after a long hike   I walked
lightly   feeling so much had owned me

rather then me owning it
my arms free   to receive
to hold   to love   anew

* G.K. Chesterton

new bush track

moving house means searching
for new wilderness
like a miner for an elusive air pocket

following a green area on a map
hidden by development
encroached to the edge
behind an old scout hall
a brambly track
winds me down
through a sandstone escarpment

the dawn sun plays into the hands
of eucalypts stretched
to seek the light   yet their search for meaning
being found more in their roots
symbiotically curled around sturdy rock

here dew-tipped casuarinas sparkle
here grass trees verdantly splurge
as if their whole purpose is to shine

self-important   the palms push upwards
screaming rock stars
honey birds swing on rusty-gold banksia
magpies warble
in the whip-cracked air

this is the Australian bush
how it pulls me in

through the trees i glimpse a waterfall
and marvel to think it has always been here
carving musically into the heart of the earth
it has sung its song for aeons

it is the human in me that delights
nature just is
in its own world
whole unto itself
it doesn't even know I'm here

and there is a loneliness in this
yet lost from the world
i am found
and to the cadence of nature
i dance

traces of you

for our millie 2000–2014

there is panic
the last night in the old house
how will i find you

here i still have the sound of creaks in the hallway
your patient sighs near my desk
urging me out for a walk
and your big dreamy eyes gazing up at me

here i have the feeling of emptiness with your absence
from the side gate each time i return home
and your presence
around corners on our familiar bush tracks

ah   you know

during the night your steady breathing wakes me
you   curled on the floor
at the side of the bed
have come back one last time

my hand drifts down
fingers play through your hair
as though I'm caressing strings of a golden harp
its music lulls me back to sleep and I wake
to the new day
and feel your energy in the dawn
in the friskiness of day
and in me

first morning in our new home

for Michael

from my fumbling first sleep
I awake before dawn

out our new window
a full sky
sparkling space station
twinkle of the morning star

and a rising smiling slither of moon
shining in on your face

disorientation melts away

Lie of the Land

lie of the land

inspired by installation of Fiona Foley

blankets   twenty pairs

flour   ten bags

knives and thirty tomahawks

treaty done

with the Wurundjeri people

they walk the white travellers around
thinking they were passing through
point out their grasslands readying for next season
show them their waterholes

forgotten warriors

history defines itself
sings legends of the frontier
explorers   stockmen   squatters
bushrangers   diggers   pioneers

yet there is a waiting
beyond our consciousness
the other side of this frontier

the first peoples of our nation
their story in the bones of the land
wait for recognition

unknown numbers
chilled the spines of the intruders
skills honed for survival over aeons
shape-shifting oneness with the bush
theirs was the sacrifice

courage outgunned

here became warriors
defending their country
their way of life   their lore

we revere fallen warriors
emblazon 'lest we forget'
on cenotaphs and memorials

is it a dark forgetting
as one forgets burning stars in daytime

is silence a denial of history

dare we disturb our complacency
find cracks   let the light shine in

Multuggerah

the weather cools
driving up the range to Toowoomba

the wind strutting itself in a showery flounce
makes every head of hair unruly
enjoys its fling
leaves flounder
bark peels like masks
falling

at the lookout
on the highest ancient volcanic point
it was only fitting to be sashayed this way and that
while reading a plaque
Multuggerah and the Battle of One Tree Hill

on this flat tabletop mountain   Multuggerah
his spiritual duty to defend his country
and the Jagera people
made his last stand

excess beauty of landscape
the great dividing range below
and vibrance of the Darling Downs
cannot redact history

battle of Richmond Hill

some of the local Darug clan
invite me

on a cold june morning
we meet in a hospital car park
walk along an overgrown path

a small memorial above the river bank
an unkempt garden   a rock   a plaque
wild red geranium amid paspalum

sandbars now swallow the flow
of this once rich food bowl
wild blackberry bush tangles

yet for those who know   the air cries
with the land   blood soaked and sacred

a gossip of magpies remain when we arrive
to forage in the long grass
eavesdroppers   listening to the story

we remember the forgetting

a smoking ceremony brings us here
sorrow grasps the moment
speech is measured by silence
cleansing smoke of eucalypt leaves
floats on a moan of wind

first executions in Melbourne

already a hot haze ascends
january heat trapped in the market square
crowded with six thousand people

Peevuy's strong young body trembles
Jack stands calm and stoic
their dark skin   incongruent in white British garb
white stockings and caps

in chains with a heavy military escort
the sentence was death by hanging

they had known the massacre of their families
Jack as a young boy watched his parents shot
in the Cape Grim surprise massacre

as proud warriors they had used guerrilla war
against the colonists
for their people and land in *lutruwita**
they evaded three military expeditions
sent to round them up

now at an inexpertly built gallows
a hush fell as they were pushed
with hands chained behind their backs
onto makeshift ladders
and ascended clinging with knees and chin

Jack of Cape Grim and Peevuy**
were executed   struggling in terror
after a second attempt into screaming silence
with the cry   *shame*   from some of the crowd

the men were left hanging
their women begging for the bodies***

they were buried
in a hole covered with lime
outside the cemetery wall
where the Melbourne Markets now stand

* *Lutruwita*: indigenous word for Tasmania

** Tunnerminnerwait and Maulboyheenner were their Indigenous names.

*** The three women of the gang, Trugannini, Planobeena and Pyterruner, were forcibly removed to Wybalenna on Flinders Island. There later, they were, with a few others, influential in orchestrating the earliest known petition to the British sovereign in 1846.

Jandamarra

Tunnel Creek in Winjana Gorge
the Kimberley outback
land of the Banuba people
the time is late nineteenth century
the last stage of white invasion
being played out
herds of cattle trample the grasses
waterholes gone
spirit broken

faded sepia shots capture   for history
naked black men with ankle and neck chains
on track to Derby lock-up
contained en route
in a thousand-year-old hollow boab tree

yet one warrior
Jandamarra takes a last stand
turns against his white masters
fights heroically
to save his people
and his country

a mythical figure he appeared   fought
disappeared   unable to be tracked
for years he held out
the one burning flame

betrayal and a bullet
a fight that died
in his Tunnel Creek cave
Jini his mother held him as life ebbed out
a pietà on the rock of Golgotha

Requiem for Bees

where have the tiny birds gone

the place i wrote my first poetry
a pocket of bush beyond a dead-end street
is gone

once ferns bathed in a small creek
carved around sandstone
orange berries of lilly pilly in winter
yellow grevilleas in spring
garden escapees vine-covered scrub
honeysuckle   morning glory
food and shelter for birds

how my heart *in hiding stirred for a bird* *
tiny acrobats in brambly undergrowth
in a hush of solitude

there was a fallen log
that made the perfect place to sit
here with my love of the romantic poets
being studied at school
i wrote pages of poetry in their style

a busy street goes
where my log once was
tiny birds have disappeared
treasured writings   lost in a flood

* G.M. Hopkins, 'Windhover'

lamentation

the old tree
is being cut down

its leaf ruffled song
a lamentation
only spindly foliage now
strangled slowly
by the hard tarred surface
concrete pebbled surrounds
and a moaning overpass
blocking sunlight

twin arms high up   stretch
supplicating the divas
will fall easily to chainsaw and crane

the main trunk is a formidable presence
silence will come
only after an horrific scream of defiance

bulging roots thrust out
they strive to hold their sense of place

progress wins against protest

remembering

funeral over
people gone
condolences done
back to routine
alone

slumped on the grass
feeling the earth
i supervise the blue team
at the swimming carnival
in the shade of the callistemon

a gentle hum
sings my senses awake
the bush is alive

how dare the world go on when i have stopped

i smile
remembering
how she would love this show of nature

bush singing to me
as bees fluster
giving the candle-red callistemon   wings

heart song

national park
banksia   acacia
melaleuca   coral heath
wild flowers and fruits
flirt

small birds
wings fluted   radar-edged
flash red   blue   yellow
burnished gold
flirt

song
lifts the air
lifts my thoughts

i drive back from the Blue Mountains
sticker on my car
no bush no birds

hours later
i'm back in the city
heart still singing

in search of Hildegard of Bingen

i take a train out of Bingen
through the Rhine Valley
on this summer day
trek up a steep hill
relieved to find an old sign   *klosterruine*
which points to a verdant track
into a cool shady grove

here remnants of the twelfth-century monastery
moss-mottled stone walls
mostly buried by vines
and embedded tree roots
is Hildegard's world

standing in this moment
with the outlines of another world
time is shapeless
the divide of centuries a blur

only my mind's eye can see
a spirited young woman
and flourishing herb garden

she prepares salves and tonics
attends the sick
listens to the breeze
and finds God in the hills above her

Kairos time
for her visions   writings   mandalas and music
later a powerful feminist voice
against corruption   patriarchy and senseless war

the earth is our mother   she would sing
revere and care for her
if we exploit and savage her
she will be out of balance
and the price will be high

then silence for nine hundred years

in our time
the scales are tipped loudly out of balance
the *all ords* and the *dow* are the measure
a daily intake of massacres crowds our entertainment
soul mutilation makes soldiers unable to cry

i lean against the wall marked Hildegard's cloister
in the lush shade of an almond tree
hanging fruit   voluptuous now
is falling to emptiness
the void
the nothingness
how human to fear the waiting
for fullness to return

scattered around me
are rotting almond fruits
flies enjoying their feast
the decay   fodder for the soil

my eyes scan for her presence

a maiden hair fern
grooved into a crumbling niche
catches my eye
delicate and tenacious
I feel a quickening
like a first flutter of new life

too often the fragile   the intimate whisper
the lightness of touch
the flicker of a sanctuary lamp
like breath   are portals and easily missed

I ponder the rise and fall of my breathing
listen to the rhythmic heart beat
hear *veriditas* chants in the crumbling walls

veriditas murmurs Hildegard

Hildegard is here
I do not flinch   i expect her
nothing like the grey statue at the abbey
holding the orb and feather

her presence is intimate
light glows luminous
her arms full of herbs from the garden
and her muddy hand-made sandals
make me laugh

requiem for bees

she looks into the garden
hands rest on the keys

her music begins sweetly
moves to buzzing fortissimo
fleetingly joyful

the second movement
a slow march   subdued
sombre   quietness   diminuendo

the third movement   drifts out
sadness   softly plays
distills the emotion of lachrymose

a flight of fancy

like notes of music, a shower of summer rain thrums on the pond
the sun breaks through and a thousand spilled jewels sparkle

stand here by the pond   be the concert-goer
welcome this acoustically perfect willow-curtained auditorium

listen to its birdsong and the frogs enjoying this turn-around day
dragonflies play tiny rainbows to themselves and large possessive
goldfish saunter along in gangs.

i did not realise a pond could be so scalloped and bathed in beauty
is it a flight of fancy to wish everyone could see such a pond?

Counting Dead Women

forgotten children

they draw pictures of themselves
with sad faces staring out
through wire fences
they are our refugee children
forgotten

voices that protest are muted
their words buried
a twenty-four-hour news cycle
spins on
in a country

with boundless plains to share
while the document
The Forgotten Children
about our forgotten children
is forgotten

counting dead women

i rose towards dawn
to sit by the big picture window

the sky   black as raven wings
lay still and silent
like a dark night of the soul

i was desperately seeking
some colour   some hope
upon the dark edge of the world
where sea and sky meet

yet my mind kept scribbling
names of women   words of violence

the darkness of the first news
counting dead women
blankets my heart over and over
even as the breath of dawn
spreads its radiance

common denominator

flowers   pencils   cricket bats
candles flickering and ribbons in the wind
teddy bears   chinese lanterns
a thousand paper cranes

for what

to make sense of the senseless
to stand in defiance
to make social media visible
to show we are not alone

secret history

'keeping silent about evil allows it to rise up a thousand fold'

cradled into the shoulder of a Tamil woman
the child is limp

australians were not supposed to see
157 asylum seekers file out of the ship's hull

our government installed a wire cage-like path
flanked with the heave and heft of yellow vested guards

its strange how luminous-yellow vests
give an air of authority

when will enough of us   see beyond
allow our hearts to fire and flow

or like a giant dam cracking open
will secret history burst and flood

In August 2014, 157 Tamil asylum seekers were held at sea for nearly a month. They were suddenly taken to the isolated desert detention centre of Curtin and then flown to the island 'gulag' of Nauru.

stillborn

winter darkens our land
the tree outside my window
is stark and bare
close up   new life is tightly budded

the news says
our country has turned back refugees at sea
people seeking asylum
returned to face those they flee

history like a drawbridge is pulled up
closed off
humanity is stillborn

hearts are cold
fear deadens minds

the everywoman in me weeps
for the birthing

the woman with child is weeping
the woman is every woman
if you are not weeping
ask why

fear of lack

and in time
one by one
they removed each stake from the crib

crows in the trees cried *ack ack*
and there came a wind
the people shrivelled in fear
and shouted lack lack

they built a wall
forced the sea out
wintering to a wasteland

and in time
the sky darkened
the people turned on each other
raised their fists
cried at each other *lack lack*

and in the distance they heard
a cock crow thrice

empathy

blood spills from the pen
briny seas bleach words
wordless

at dinner   TV images
toughen hearts   exhaust spirits   desensitise

ads break tension
relief comes with the *all ords* and the *dow*   up or down
who cares
as long as there are no names or clear faces
just humanity   ragged   emaciated

the screen divides   us and them
our fears   our terror cannot be sated

can our fragile
fragile globe
be saved without empathy

imagine how they feel

how would i feel   fleeing my homeland
at sea in the blackness of night
the Milky Way a glorious bridge
would the sign of the Southern Cross give hope
that someone cares and hearts may open

the fluff of a pillow   pull up of a doona
haunted by others   cold and wet

dare i imagine
the muscle of empathy   flexing
to build a new way forward

so what!

so what for poetry
stand on a corner
cry words!

they hear only heartbeats and their child's cry

give out flyers of poetic words
amidst the human chaos

no free hands
burdened down with helping each other

make my body a hangar for a billboard

they only stare ahead determinedly
for their next water   food   rest area

so what for poetry
that speaks of life and love   beauty and pain

their long struggle
one aching step following the other
is their poetry

unknown journeys   boats   roads   railway tracks
facing borders   razor wire   walls
is their poetry

their fear of where they go   crammed on buses and trains
the hope of life that drives their inner soul
is their poetry

so let my poetry
be the tears when i see those
that smile welcome
giving food and clothes and care

let my poetry be the ache in my heart
as i lie in a warm safe bed
and wonder what my poetry would be
if i were in their shoes

out of sight out of mind

what is it about islands bearing secrets
wholeness   paradise
yet in their genesis
proud fruit lurks
holding
for a fall

what is it about islands bearing secrets
maybe oceans bellow a pounding howl
define barriers   deafen cries
pinchgut   port arthur   norfolk   sarah
flinders   rottnest
all bear secrets
now dark history

what is it about islands bearing secrets
out of sight   out of mind
christmas   manus   nauru
ripe for the plucking
yet their fruit is hard to digest   gulag-tough
bearing secrets

please call me by my name

visions crack like leaves in street gutters
wire fencing gashes at hearts
people listless and bored
imprisoned on sweaty islands

please call me by my own name
so i can hear myself cry

leaders spruik terror
backs turn
long nights   long days

is 'rot in hell' the way
to fuel the furnace of politics

we are sorry

there will come a time
when we bring these young ones
home from oblivion
name them
declare their age and their home of birth
admire and respect them
for their courage in their plight

if only we had the national imagination
and the heart
to do it now

for it will come to pass
a leader stands and exclaims
we are sorry for those who suffered
from our pacific solution
from their time on christmas island
from their forced stay on manus
for the damage done   gaoled on nauru
we are sorry about the temporary protection visa
for the policy of no visa
for the tough and mean treatment at our hands
in your moment of most desperate plight.

and the people now scarred
by loss of homelands
and the dash of hope they held

will look up
listen
and struggle on

the wrong side of the track

it was just a thought as i passed
an old rags and tatters fig tree
with plastic-sleeved notice nailed to its girth
notification of tree removal and replacement

if planted a few metres further over
it would be the other side of the stonewall
with botanical garden privilege
no groaning expressway blocking its light
no compressed cement
strangling its bulging roots

here it is the victim
on the wrong side of the track

doctors without borders don't worry about sides
organic farms struggle with boundaries
and radiation fallout drifts carelessly

those who have fled homelands
and face walls and wire fences
look up   watch a bird fly
long to be on the other side

on the next walk down macquarie street
from the library to the quay
absence of the old battler fig
cries for what is gone.

hydra

a giant immortal beast
once buried
long ago
stirs

at first a shadow

its fiery breath poisons hearts
ignites minds

its whisper of vengeance
becomes a chorus
crescendos to revenge

hercules' struggle to rid the land
finds each hydra head cut down
rears up double
is forgotten
and a cry in the wilderness
revenge is not the way   is just a cry

with an industry of weapons
enterprise for breakdown
innocent blood flows

in forgetfulness
heads rearing up are named
knocked down like a pack of cards
but again they multiply

amidst the chaos a prophet's words
darkness cannot drive out darkness*
blows on the wind

fears build walls to hide the cracks
different gods are invoked
many kill for their god
many die for their god
as mothers weep and babies cry
an old man sits against a destroyed wall
stares into the future

from a crack in the wall
a red geranium
can only speak if someone listens

and the young look on

---

* Martin Luther King Jr, 1967

christmas is over

i see people being killed
by two suicide bombers
in the market place
near Bethlehem

Christmas is over
for another year
our remotes are not working
all the double As are needed
for the toys

there is colour from the distance
a river of humanity floods along
it is when the camera pans in
you see the faces
anguish   fear
freezing cold children
hear their cries

christmas decorations are packed away
the church crib boxed for another year

Eagle Wings

on becoming a grandparent

there are no words
only movement through me

sculpture
of your tiny pink ear whorls
like ocean waves
mystery deep

toes curve like cowrie shells
precious treasure from the sea

your wrinkled skin silken-soft
smells of milky love

your breath
feather light claims life

when your eyes open   aquamarine
there is a sea-sun sparkle
dazlious in your distant ancient gaze

your tiny hand curls around my little finger
and enfolds me tenaciously

the first time I hold you

distant grandparenting

you give me smiles and lullabies
you give me clapping hands
and twinkle twinkle little star

i watch your first steps
and your play
share your books
and catch the light in your eyes

you give me joy
when you toddle towards me
with a smile and arms outstretched
when your tiny hand reaches towards the computer
when you blur in to kiss me on the screen

but Skype does not give me a cuddle
nor let me feel your hand
tiny and warm and curved in mine

3 moments at Heathrow

at Heathrow airport
eyes light up
a summer moment

when a long-distant grandchild
smiles recognition
i give thanks for Skype

daughter in your arms
and a precious one inside
visitation

spirit guide

many times I have met her while out walking
her voice is snappy
you can do it she would say
you can be strong
come each day
we will do it together
greet me with the stamp of your foot
hit your right fist into your left palm
look me in the eye

look this fragmented world in the eye
always through the prism of light
through every spectrum
grasp it
with your whole being
even as it wounds you
live this precious thing called life
remember to breathe it

i take a deep breath
my first deep breath

have i been living underwater all my life
like a rubber ball   held down
released   i explode to the surface

the breath is sweet
its awareness assuages me

she wears red shorts
affirms me
takes things lightly
and laughs with the chuckle of kookaburras

as i was leaving
she asked me to remember
what she had taught me

i took a deep breath
stamped my foot on the ground
hit my right fist into the palm of my left hand
looked her in the eye   breathed deeply

suddenly we were one
one voice
shouting
yes   yes   that's it

witness

i remember
when i realised i was there
watching myself

slowly i came to know the watcher

sometimes i feel us clearly
me with her
her with me

i feel her watching me
and i watch her watch
how i react

i like it when she whispers
we can do it
and then I know we can

refuge

it smells so good
the cafe   a comfort
from the storming

sitting here
pondering the smooth
sax of Kenny G

the colour tastes just right
awaiting my latte
and apple friand

weeping day

slow lull of morning
yawns sleepily
wrinkly clouds sag

my anchored body
craves a cave
to hide from this day

out my window
the honeysuckle
lilts cheekily over the fence

yes it is reckless
is called noxious
sentenced to be eradicated

but it thrives
reassures me with its smile
and nods *yes* to life
on this weeping day

eagle wings

i walk from the hospital
choose the stairs over the lift

all six floors of them
and count down

litany of numbers
moaned under my breath
with devotion

then with crescendo
madly   loudly

fear morphs into wings
eagle wings

their wide span
awhoosh awhoosh

from high on the mountain
there is such beauty

i weep

claustrophobic

if a tree falls in a forest
and no one is around   does it make a sound

we wondered as we decorated the cedar
where the magpies sit at dawn
to wake us with their morning warble

if we decorated a tree in a forest
with coloured lights would they shine
if there was no one around to see them

we felt like the child trying to see
if the light was still on
when the fridge door is closed

now I ask   sitting here at my desk
is this room an ocean

am I awash
with electronic waves
even when i'm not tuned in

waking to day

sometimes   light breaks in
with pickaxe sharpness

tucked in undercover dreams
eyes shut tight

i begin to follow threads
into a minotaur-morning

sometimes   light breaks in
a knight in shining armour

a rescue   from a night of terrors
eyes fly open

relieved   i fling off fear
into a billowing-sail morning

we dress to mask the other
and step out to face the day

bucket list

this isn't on our bucket list
michael says
as we enter Westmead hospital
no   this is so we can get on with it I say

but how has it come to this
our conversation   of doctors and dentists
of walkers and railings and ramps
all of a sudden this is it

friends with medical worries
even dying creeps closer
not long ago the words retirement
seniors   super   pensions were remote

we talk of down sizing
things seeing us out
sudoku for our minds and U3A
even of retirement villages

we see the humour
in *the best exotic marigold hotel*
and get the ageing jokes
yet I feel no different

the pink bounce of evening dusk
lingers in my heart
long after dark

funeral for a lover of Italian travel

it's come down to this
like a hit to the shin
my sense of control
is out of control
becoming raw illusion

time is expensive
music for arrival
summaries of a life
each slotted and timed to fit in

a significant song
today Bocelli's '*Con te partiro*'
for a lover of Italian travel
a cup of tea   gourmet sandwich

there are more and more funerals
great to get back home
where my camellias flourish

Exultation

parallel realms

just before dusk   the light still playful
our tents already settled
a lily-studded lagoon begins to dim

if I had been at home in the city
i'd be about the billions spent
on the chill of submarines
protesting someone's grandchild drowning in them
who now struggles to learn in the heat
of a demountable classroom

if i had been in Sydney
i'd be writing against inhumanity
denying words like *irregular maritime arrivals*

here   is theatre of another kind
curtain has risen
for an operatic show   wading black-necked jabirus
forage
throw their heads back as if in delight

their spindly coral-red legs
choreographed to water music
dance   lift off
fan-like wings hover
linger on the air's wedge
and then become silhouettes of the sun
as silence surges in

this realm is enough for me
sometimes i wish there were no portal back
then again   i am not needed here

not narcissus

it isn't really what he says
it's the way his voice   like waves
wash over the spread of my mind

how his breath catches
like the wood pigeon on wing

how his touch like dipping branches
of the willow in the pond
sends ripples into my every cell

it's the way his warmth like red wine
flows into the pockets of my heart

how his face brims with delight
when he speaks of our grandchildren
and how his eyes hold mine
mirroring my reflection as beautiful and loved

taking wings

if ever there was a summer day so perfect
so romantic under its mild autumn sun
constantly making love to the trees and flowers

that it made you wish to tear at your shackles
rip off your yoke
feel exposed to its sharp pinion

and to give yourself over to brash colour
without an iota of worry

a day that made you pack a sandwich
and with a bottle of water to set out

to walk quiet ways catching the song
of tiny birds brimming in wild blackberry brambles

and for a moment feel your heart sing
with even just a quaver of gratitude

well today is just that kind of day*

* after Billy Collins

choice

sometimes you can wait a long time for the bus
like waiting for life

advertisements in the bus shelter catch your waiting
defame your chance for that state of bliss

you wait in noise   inhale gas emissions of a city jungle
and between your fingers the opal card rests

you wait for a nearly packed standing room only
cumbersome object with specific number 370

a tiny brown sparrow in the gutter defies fragility
as it tackles a twig too big for its flight

we all have baggage   often too big to balance
yet the sparrow seems unfazed

why can't she leave the twig behind and fly
let the bus pulling in   be her diversion

on the bus   you realise your direction is chosen
yet choosing means   you missed another

out the window the brown sparrow
now on the footpath still struggles with the twig

sunflowers

imagine walking along a noisy street
mind twirling like a wind-blown chime
enter a parkland
where even your footsteps
are absorbed by the grass

find yourself like alice shrunk in wonderland
before a field of sunflowers
with dawning faces like a thousand suns
fanfare of rusted gold
dressed lavishly in green

watch them turn   a slow liturgical dance
to follow the sun
and be amazed

as is their destiny
they bear nectar for bees
their seeds lined up for birds

and they stand   scarred   weather-worn
to their last crumble   crunched
dried up life cycle

they have no desires
only lush beauty
and their moment in time

the vicissitude of a blue butterfly

she lavishly opens her wings
teal-blue fan quivers
playing warm still air
motley light from the trees

she darts and dives
ah with what precision
dodges the many hazards
with angular flight

creole-eyed she alights to sip
from sweet honey-dewed
red-dressed grevilleas

moves like notes of music
up and down around and in me
with lightness and freedom

i know dull blue of wings
etherised
silver-pinned under glass

and think of shy miss butterfly
sprawled in Eliot's poem
pinned and wriggling on the wall

today her iridescent triangles of blue
flash with the sun   like flying jewels
intoxicated with life

exultation

i trek along a bush track
mostly gum-green foliage
dropped dead limbs sticks and brambles
camouflaged homes of abundant life
overgrown vines and bristly hakea
confuse the way
inhaling eucalyptus air   calms
but doesn't clear the track

i clamber up a sandstone outcrop
stand like a wedge-tailed eagle
wings outstretched
on top of the world
look down on the canopy of the gums
a red flowery secret hidden from below

exultation stirs
seizes me shakes me awake

it looks easier from on high
or is it a childhood memory
of snugglepot and cuddlepie
swaying in the breeze
or just my love of the bush

exultation is illusive
its extravagance intangible
like love you feel for someone
like a sense of wonder before beauty

back on the track
the way feels different

autumnal music

i thought i knew the sound
its rustic ring
its tingle
down
my spine
its warm gurgle in my feet

and hands
its whisper
at the nape of my neck
and satisfying sighs pulsing
cool and crisp and clear

yet autumn always shocks
its soul-satisfying crunches
and munches and moans
wild wind in corridors
and howls through window gaps

its rhyming rustle tones
with snicks and snaps and cracks
always surprise
as I listen
to the easy drift of vesper leaves
settling to a hush

red sirens

bees deep in the bush
bright red waratahs
lure them in

for a moment

sometimes we have to wait
a space
a time
an openness

sometimes it takes expansiveness
of landscape
the big blues of sea and sky
a reminder of inner spaciousness
to touch something deeper
that stirs
quietly

above the horizon silver gulls
a curving streak   morph
into a thousand swirls and hurls
and dips
a shock and shimmer of light
a fluster over a shoal of fish
the mass of water
under splash of wing   flickers   flashes
transforming exuberance

we can miss it
yet if we wait
edges meld
as a meniscus giving way

and nature seeps in
for a moment

wood pigeon

for yana

the glass door shuddered
a chill shot down my spine
a wood pigeon lay on the door step
i picked it up
cupped it in my two hands like this
alert to its rapid heartbeat

ah the intimacy i felt
close to this normally aloof bird
i comforted its warm plump body
cooed to it like a bird whisperer
no way as serenely as it does to me
in the red-berried puriri tree at dusk

it stayed dazed for a short time
then slowly lifted its head as i stroked
down its iridescent green feathers
i like to think it felt safe

wings opened to full exquisite span
and from my hands it took flight

i thought as i watched it go free
what a privilege it was to hold
such beauty and strength
in my hands

in our garden

thieves of the night

under an ace-black sky
free loaders
crunch   munch
midnight feast
freshly planted herb garden

caught

quiet of evening
after tea
rustle rustle thump thump
back for more
four shiny eyes stare down

old violin

eyes follow a plume of dust
as a violin is plucked
from its bruised black case

*what have we here
an old violin seen better days
any bids*

the audience tunes out
the auctioneer holds it high
the room is restlessly quiet

through the muffled air
from the back of the crowd
someone shuffles forward

she reaches out   strokes its wood
her knowing hands tighten strings
then tucks it under her chin

music fills the air
with commanding presence
hearts sigh deeply

and now what am i bid
the auctioneer calls
hands rise around the room

visitor

closer
trust

silently
listen

amazed
by jewels of

song
tell me

slowly again
you are joy

Rostropovich

written on hearing of his passing

life   maestro   still sings through your strings
timeless   lifting us from our tattered
mind into a tapestry of hope

your hands transcend the pain
in an alien land   o exiled one
how your passion stirs humanity

far from your beloved homeland
your music silences the screams that rage
against the spark of freedom denied

your cello melts to memory
crumbling stone   the rampart wall of death
and stills the heart of division

strings weep wistful tears   cleanse minds
as evening dew lightly on leaves washes
the day's grime

death   maestro   a farewell crowned
with laurels   your heavenly cello plays
they stand as you pass   hands busy clapping

cannot wipe tears   flowers cover the earth
shared with wood and strings
there are no words   just the music

Slavo Rostropovich 1927–2007

unexpected visitor

clinging to the inside of a coffee mug
left on the terrace overnight
googled eyes on a pin-sized head
scan me

shiver of greenish brown body   touch of orange
grasping stick legs
and long fine feelers
all aquiver
swaying waving into emptiness
touching   touching air

and its wings   its wings alight with dawn
transparent beauty
candescent

had it fallen in
trembled all night in the dark

we know how it feels
we who have felt helpless

the fragility of a dragonfly
grasping to get a hold
to launch on arched angelic wings
away from despair

a frisson of love stirs my heart
what courage   what energy
it takes
even with a helping hand
to get out of the coffee dregs

a poem of instruction

on how to move forward in chaotic times

tread slowly
feel the earth sacred beneath you
respect her for she nourishes and protects you
allow her riffle of welcome to hold you

be open to the blessings so easily smothered
in the busyness
that comes up to meet you every day

use soft gaze to receive
the beauty of the natural in a chaotic world
know this is your life
hold it all lightly
to the quiet centre of your being

listen to your heart
its beat is ancient wisdom speaking
too often we suppress it
too easily we silence it
do not be afraid to hear its murmurings
it is your guide

remember to breathe
how precious is the breath
its struggle   first to last
our life force

do not lose track of the world
hold firmly your laughter   your dance   your song
your inner peace

be aware of life's blessings
receive them with gratitude

and be awake
stay awake
let your voice be heard

this is the journey
one step at a time

www.ingramcontent.com/pod-product-compliance
Lightning Source LLC
Chambersburg PA
CBHW070919080526
44589CB00013B/1371